DIARY OF A ROSE LOVER

BY HENRI DELBARD

Watercolors by Fabrice Moireau

Harry N. Abrams, Inc., Publishers

Two like-minded people joined in writing
and illustrating this notebook during
the summer of 1994 at the village of
Malicorne, in the centre of France.
Of course none of this would have come about
if I had not been born nearby in 1944,
surrounded by roses, sharing with my two
brothers, François and Guy, our parents'
love and their passion for nature.

During the time I was writing this book, the roguish
and eager smile of my late son Benoît never
left me. I dedicate this book to his brothers and to all
children, the gardeners of tomorrow's world.

Roses have much to tell us! This is a lesson I learned from that great humanist, Henri Charnay, who one day unlocked my heart and mind, and to Jacques Puisais, Monique Schlienger and Jean-Philippe Lenclos, who taught me how to use my senses.

If you will come along with me, we shall see, smell, taste, touch and perhaps even hear the happiness that the roses in our gardens can bring to us. But first you have to learn to understand, through understanding to recognize, and through recognition to love. That's the idea behind this instruction in pleasure that I hope to share with you.

The Colours of Roses

The language of colour has an alphabet based on the colour-wheel:
six colours, three of them warm – red, orange, yellow – and three
of them cool – green, blue, violet. Starting from there,
everything is simple!

– First of all, choose your temperature.
Do you prefer warm colours to cool ones?
Your answer will enable you to specify the basic colour
that gives you the greatest pleasure. But in most cases,
a garden will not consist of a single colour. So you will
want to learn about combinations. Ask yourself this
second question: Do I like combinations to be strong ones
or mild? In accordance with your answer, the colour-wheel will show you
the possibilities.

Say you went for mildness. Then, starting
with the basic colour you chose in
response to the first question, you will
have to mix it with the nearest
colours on the wheel.
For example, green or
violet can be combined
with blue; the result
will be cool and mild, no matter which of
the colours you emphasize.

1

2

Mild contrast : 1 - with warm colours
                   2 - with cool colours

If you incline towards strong contrast, combine diametrically opposite colours on the wheel. These are called "complementary". The result is a contrasting effect, each opposite colour putting the other into relief. But in this case, since you are using both cool and warm colours, you will have to measure them out and

Strong contrast :
1 - predominantly warm
2 - predominantly cool

emphasize the colour whose "temperature" you preferred at the outset.

Obviously this approach can be elaborated into infinity, particularly in dealing with the brightness or darkness of the colours. The easiest, and often the happiest unions are achieved between those of the same brightness or of the same darkness.

White can be used along with one or more colours that you may want to enhance. In certain contexts, it will provide lightness and liveliness.

Blue, the colour of sea and sky, the colour of space, is used to give depth. It extends the horizon, and unites the earth and the sky.

Red, the colour of blood and embers, stimulates the senses and draws the attention. It marks out the perspectives and views that you want to stress.

Yellow, the colour of the sun, warms and illuminates. Few gardeners think of yellow to brighten up a dark, inhospitable corner, and yet there are many plants with yellow flowers or leaves.

Green calms, cools and refreshes, and links together the other colours of the garden. What delight to bask in greenery !

3

The scents of roses

Roses offer us an infinite variety of scents : each has its own, as easy to recognize as a famous brand of perfume. Monique Schlienger, a professional "nose" and a wonderful instructor, taught me that all scents are an assemblage of natural olfactory notes : lavender, citronella, peach, lilac, cedar, jasmine, etc...
And the most volatile notes — those that we smell first — belong to two families, the citrus and the aromatic ; they are the most fleeting and constitute the " head" notes of the perfume.
This is the perfume's spirit.
   Then come the notes of flowers, fruit, spices and plants. These are the perfume's heart, its personality. These soon give way to the lower, heavier components, which form the wake of the perfume with the deep and lasting notes : wood and balsam.
Thus I devised with Schlienger a method of representing the structure of a rose's scent, an actual " olfactory landscape". By using this technique of representing each olfactory family by a colour, we can visualize the scent of every rose !   But you also have to know how to smell. Smelling requires a great deal of calm and concentration. Begin with a " first sniff", no more than a few seconds, lest your hypersensitive olfactory cells become anaesthetized. After that, memory has to go to work. In your personal collection of scents there must be something similar. Think first of the most volatile notes. Savouring and comparing the scent of two or three roses at one time often helps to speed things up.
Thus it's a good idea to begin with a rose that has the least intense scent.

Do all roses have a scent?

Aside from a few rare examples, the answer is yes. All you need is a bit of patience and above all to keep in mind that, like all living things, a rose has an internal clock. That is, it lives by its own rhythm, which depends on the flower's stage of development, the time of day and the weather conditions.

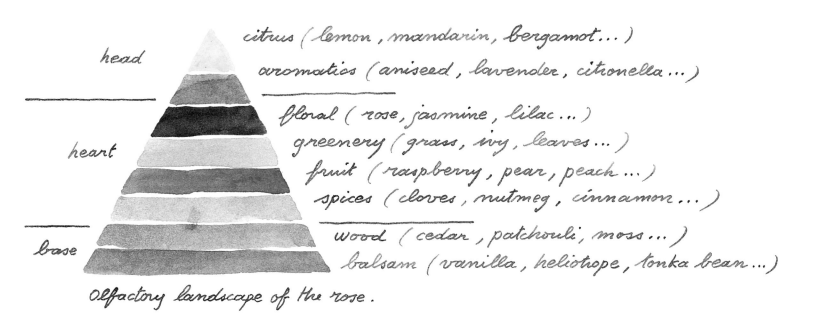

head
heart
base

citrus (lemon, mandarin, bergamot...)
aromatics (aniseed, lavender, citronella...)

floral (rose, jasmine, lilac...)
greenery (grass, ivy, leaves...)
fruit (raspberry, pear, peach...)
spices (cloves, nutmeg, cinnamon...)

wood (cedar, patchouli, moss...)
balsam (vanilla, heliotrope, tonka bean...)

Olfactory landscape of the rose.

New techniques for analyzing the molecules given off by roses ("head space") have shown that it takes almost twelve hours for a rose to play all its notes. In this way the intensity as well as the composition of its scents varies in the course of the day. So if a rose seems to have no scent, maybe it is tired. Return a little later and it will speak to you!

"Grand Siècle"

It should also be noted that, to diffuse their scent, roses require a certain temperature (18-20°c is the optimum) as well as a certain humidity. Beware of the parasitic odours of tobacco, personal perfume and the like...

   After the rose has been in a vase for some time, the scent may change, and in the morning you have to wait for the temperature to rise before the rose expresses its deepest notes.

   Generally speaking, on a plant the half-open and most intensely coloured blossoms will have the strongest scent. That's certainly the case with "Grand Siècle".

scent

rose
apple
raspberry.

"Grand Siècle"

The quintessential rose!
Feminine, elegant, beautiful,
a true rose colour, exceptionally rich.
I always begin a "tasting" of scents with "Grand Siècle" because of its
predominantly floral perfume. Our senses operate by comparison, and in
the case of smell, as in hearing, you need to know "middle c".
"Grand Siècle" gives me my pitch, and to discover other scents, I first of all
tune my nose to the "rose" key. Of course, it is not only rose, that would be dull!
But you will see that its other notes of raspberry and apple are easy to iden-
tify and separate. It would be difficult to conceive of a rose-garden
without "Grand Siècle", which was awarded the gold medal at the
Paris Bagatelle Exhibition, as well as the Manuel Canovas prize.

7

"Fêtes Galantes"

A worthy daughter of "Grand Siècle",
with the same presence, the same perfection,
she perpetuates the tradition of elegance and
beauty. She is also love, the warmth of
seduction and the royal purple of
ceremony.

"Fêtes Galantes" seems to
have been designed to
go with a grand dinner
or just a tête-à-tête.
Her scent has only
heart notes :
rose to charm,
raspberry to
savour.
Who can resist ?

rose
raspberry
scent

8

Assembly room

Versailles,
the Marble court
8 July 1991

9.

Roses are hermaphrodites, possessing both male and female organs. They are usually united thanks to the wind, but they also bring into play the most sophisticated techniques of cosmetics in order to attract the pollen-bearing bees.

At the Delbard Nurseries, my brother Guy supervises these matings, for he understands the language of roses. He will not divulge his secret wisdom, but experience has taught him that the parent chosen to be the female generally supplies the vigour and the male transmits the colour and scent of their offspring.

The flower selected as the male is stripped of its petals, and the pollen carefully collected.
After the petals and stamens of the flower that will be the female are removed, all that remains is to deposit the pollen, the male's semen, on its pistil.

When the marriage is consummated
and the flower impregnated, it is
covered with a hood of rolled
newspaper. In the autumn the
rose-hips, the fruit of this
conjunction, redden and swell.
    They will be gathered at the begin-
ning of winter and the seeds will be removed
from their casing.
In the first days of January, the seeds are sown in
rows, and come spring the first timid rays of the sun
will warm the nascent seedlings.

11

The baby roses are about to burst into bloom.
Some will have the most amazing colours!

This adorable little rose with its finely
sculptured petals was first observed in July 1994.

Like "Harlequin", this rose, dressed at birth in green
sepals, will change its costume at every stage of its life.
New roses like this will be studied for three to five years.

"Souvenirs d'Amour"

These roses, voluptuous, romantic, unique in their charm, express the sensitivity and tradition of French gardening.

"Comtesse de Ségur"

This rose always puts me in mind of an old and very beautiful lady with finely chiselled wrinkles in her face. She radiates a sense of generosity; she wants to give everything she can to her grandchildren, and has risen early in the morning to gather a basket of roses for them. As the mischievous imps, their cheeks smeared with jam, ready themselves for the day ahead, she sets down this basket amid bowls of coffee and toast, pushing aside the pots of red currant and raspberry preserves.

She has just come from the sun, and there are a few drops of dew on her upper lip and her forehead. She smells of the morning and the first odours awakened by the sun ...

There is an odd resemblance between these roses, with their masses of short petals forming a whole series of crests and hollows, and the wrinkles that mark this loving grandmother's face.

"How wonderful these
roses smell !" the
children exclaim.
"Like raspberries or
strawberries, or maybe
even apricots" and then the
youngest points out that their colour
is the same as her dress !
And the children will remember
forever this moment of sweetness, harmony
and happiness, like a memory of love.

"Souvenir de Marcel Proust", "Comtesse de Ségur"
and the two marvellous roses that come next
remind me of those moments of happiness.

rose

raspberry, strawberry
apricot.

scent

15

" Chartreuse de Parme "... with
flowers like a preserve made of very
ripe bilberries. Its broad bluish
leaves are like a compote dish.
Perfume cup at international new roses
competitions 1996 : Paris-Bagatelle, Madrid,
Geneva and Baden-Baden.

tangerine
citronella
hyacinth, lilac
passion fruit, mango, litchi

scent

Rose gardens and berries

Unique among flowers, roses offer a varied range of colours and scents.
On a friend's suggestion, I have used this versatility to combine roses
with small fruits which are of the same size and similar leaves. As they
mature before the roses do, the aroma of bilberries, blackberries,
gooseberries and black currants remain in our memory and signal to us
the blossoming of the roses. But before that happens, these berries will
have delicately deposited the benefit of their flavour on the rose buds.

Souvenir d'Amour "Dragée" (Sugared almonds),
a bride's rose with an unforgettable scent.
Selected in July 1994.

scent

citronella
rose
peach, apricot,
pear

" Souvenir de Marcel Proust "

    With this noble, maternal rose you will rediscover the emotions of your
early childhood. Its colour is certainly warm and embracing, but it
is the scent which will convey you back to childhood.
It is well-known that an odour can revive a long-lost memory, such
as a place or a piece of music which may reappear as if by magic...

A change of key : painters' roses take the
place of memories of love...

"Souvenir de
Marcel Proust"

"Claude Monet"

Just as Proust
was moved by
a piece of madeleine
cake dipped in tea, the scent of this
"Claude Monet" rose invites you to stroll in the
garden of your childhood. In the morning, it's
the herb-garden with its notes of citronella, at noon
the orchard with its odours of pear, peach, apricots, and
in the evening the notes of sandalwood and cedar will lead
you among the trees.

citronella
pear, apricot
cinnamon
sandalwood,
cedar

scent

Painters' roses

In 1986, I had one of the most wonderful experiences of my life. I had recently taken over the management of one of the largest rose nurseries in California. While strolling through the extensive trial beds of new varieties, my attention was suddenly seized by the roses that you are about to discover. I was struck, indeed spellbound, by the colour combinations spread before my eyes. When I asked the hybridizer and the marketing staff about them, I was told that they did not look like roses! (The same view, incidentally, was taken on the other side of the Atlantic.)

Soon afterwards, I returned to Paris for a brief visit. The Musée d'Orsay in Paris had just opened and I hastened to see the inaugural exhibition of Impressionist and Post-Impressionist masterpieces. And there I had a shock in finding a random but definite link between the colours in those paintings and the colours of the roses that had seduced me in California.

"Claude Monet"

bergamot, lemon
rose
pear, vine-peach
green almond, ivy
scent   vanilla

A rose with white, red, yellow tongues of flame. A bud may burst in crimson and that shade will soften as the other colours come to life.

Monet worked on constantly changing effects, like this rose whose colours vary from one flower to the next. He would have loved to add it to his garden in Giverny.

This is a garden rose, but happily it can also be found in some good florists' shops.

Ancinet, 12 July 1994
10.30 p.m.

Stubborn as I am, it still took me almost six years to finally present the new collection of artists' roses, because in our world of gardeners, those who shared my vision were few. But once again chance came to my rescue. After having worked in 1989 and 1990 with a number of artists, philosophers and experts in tastes and smells, I decided in 1991 to concentrate on colours in order to achieve my dream of becoming a "gardener of five senses"!

On one occasion, my hand fell by accident on the catalogue of the Impressionist exhibition at the Musée d'Orsay. I read the introduction by the gifted writer and art critic Edward Lucie-Smith. All at once everything became crystal clear to me. My roses had really been created in the Impressionist style! To quote Lucie-Smith: "The Impressionists used little touches of pure colour; these mingled and produced the desired colour only when the painting was seen from a certain distance."

I leapt to the telephone, and Ted came to Paris the very next day. Excitedly I asked him whether my roses were not "painted" in the Impressionist manner. His response was not just positive, but emphatic. He then helped me in the search for an artist's name for each of my roses...

22

"Paul Gauguin"

Afterwards
this project was
supported by many
artists and intellectuals.
The Institut de France gave me permission
to name one of the roses Claude Monet. This was
soon to adorn the refurbished gardens of the
Musée Marmottan in Paris, where the most
important collection of Monet paintings is housed.

"Paul Gauguin"
Reds and violets, the colours of vine-peach, raspberries
and wine lees along the edges of the leaves follow
an irregular but harmonious order of soft white
and pink splashes. From the buds to the flowers,
a "Gauguin" bush in your garden will prove
an unforgettable sight.

23

carnation
clove
scent   vanilla

Malicorne , 13 July 94

24

orange
pear, orgeat
cinnamon

scent

"Paul Cézanne"
A palette of warm, light colours, capriciously distributed, as in some of
Cézanne's paintings, by a "random gene". The extreme sensitivity of its
vivid pigments will make this rose change according to the varying
intensity of light.

" Henri Matisse "

This rose, under the guidance
of the hybridizer, pays homage
to the colour flair of the great
Fauve painter.

raspberry
rose
scent.

The flower is all decked out in white,
pink and red, colours of crushed currants
and raspberries ; its perfume is rich
with notes of rose and raspberry.
Endearing in nature, its sole aim seems
to be to give pleasure to all gardeners
and lovers of nature.
In the autumn of 1995, this little marvel
of seductiveness was introduced into
private gardens and all the best flower
shops.

8.30 a.m.
warm
already?

The process of selection

At the end of three or four years of selection,
   only one strain in a thousand will be retained. Competition
is strong, for one strain may be particularly sturdy, another may
have the most beguiling fragrance and others may be as colourful
as playing cards. The process of choosing is rather like an
audition, with a number of examinations and evaluations.
My heart aches for those who will inevitably be eliminated.

28

"Mitsouko"

Embers smouldering in its heart
are visible through transparent
leaves like a will-o'-the wisp,
glowing red with yellow
flames or with an almost
sulphurous blue.
What strength in
this flower, even
while its wide-open
petals seem to be so
soft and gracious.
Surrounding the
flowers like
firebrands, the
young shoots are
anthocyanin red.

I prefer "Mitsouko"
to be planted in a
long border at the foot
of a light-coloured wall.
A few dewdrops bring out
its scent of freshly mown
grass, violet and raspberry.

scent   herbaceous, violet
raspberry

29

"Wild Heart"

lily of the valley, lilac
dried hay

scent

"Rebellious"

honey
beeswax
carrot-tops

scent

Sauvageonnes

- Roses selected for their wild and natural characteristics -
A new category of rose-bushes for me, these are simple, abundant in
blossom, tender in colour, with small, finely serrated leaves.
   Their exuberant, supple, rather unruly vegetation enables them
to adapt to all situations - isolated, in borders, or combined with
other stockier bushes. For instance, they are delightful among a group
of ornamental shrubs and hardy annuals such as achillea and pentstemon.
They can be pruned when they have reached the desired
height and volume.

"Rebellious"

"Wild Heart"

"Wild Heart"
Because of the softness of its
colour and scent, I choose it to accompany roses of a
strong yellow, such as "Souvenir de Marcel Proust".
They make one of the most ravishing strong cold-hot
combinations that I know.

"Rebellious"
A light, very green scent. Its branches bend under the
weight of its floral clusters. I use it to reinvigorate a
border or a corner of the garden that has gone too green.

31

"Vanilla Bouquet". It is nothing more than a bouquet of delicate flowers,

Honey
hay

scent

33

but the development of its colours from the bud to the fully open flower is astonishing.

"Lavender Dream"

I saw the child's finger
lightly brushing this
ravishing, young, frail,
tiny rose.
He sensed that it was
there for him. He had
to touch it in order to
get to know it, to
understand it.
The delicacy and
weightlessness of the
petals told him that
the rose too was a child,
playing like him in the
sun and wind.
When he went over to smell
its scent, they seemed
to be exchanging
a long kiss.
Later on, this child will
recall the lavender
colours of this rose.
But will he remember
that its scent was only
lily of the valley?

scent — lily of the valley
heliotrope

34

When mixed with "Claude Monet", "Lavender Dream"
creates a warm cameo effect of rose, red and violet.
   The yellow stamens of "Lavender Dream" and the irregular
splashes of colour in "Claude Monet" impart lightness and
warmth to this composition. The sizes of these bushes
and of their flowers are complementary, which
assures a happy union.
   Monet would not have been
displeased to see "his" rose side by
side with a "wild",
simple, graceful one
such as
"Lavender Dream".

"Lavender
Dream"

"Claude Monet"

35

rose
hay

"Raspberry Sorbet"
    Raspberry-coloured sparks on a white corolla with
bright yellow or orange stamens. A palette of gentle
shades which make it ideal for mixing with
any of the other "Sauvageonnes".

36

Malicorne.
The porch of the
XIII th - century
Romanesque church.
The view from my
father's garden.
19 July

"Raspberry Sorbet", the church of Malicorne...
Nothing in common ?   Just look! Aren't you struck by the similarity
of coloration, particularly in the violaceous pink patches, and the
shape of the porch and the rose-window? The material and the sacred
on the one hand ; life and the profane on
the other.

"Pur Caprice"

Are these flowers, or leaves?
 The flower is green and modestly melts into the foliage.
It is a strain notable for its longevity and resistance to disease.
 Observed first in July 1994.

ON THE LOOKOUT FOR EMOTIONS

Sauzet Woods

A silence full of sounds, smells and lights. Though often imperceptible, everything is moving... The slightest cloud changes the thousands of shadows cast by the foliage. The slightest breeze bears a cool perfume, a mixture of fern and honeysuckle. But always in the background is the smell of wood decomposing. Is the humidity on the increase? The odour of dead leaves, moss, peat and everything that goes into this litter takes over, a reminder that all this vegetation will inexorably return to the earth from which it sprang.

Spending countless hours perched high in this observation post, listening to nature, I learned to keep a watch out for smells, sounds and sights. Within this dense, complex landscape, I learned to detect the slightest unusual movement of a fern, which suddenly sways to a different rhythm from the one given to its companions by the wind. A few moments later, I notice the black fringe of a young doe's ear, then a hare, and for a few minutes they gambol together, running after one another. An acceleration of rhythm, a twittering, the brief call of a jay announce the arrival of an animal, and if all the sounds die down, it means a fox on the prowl. Being aware of these barely perceptible messages that only our sharpened senses can make out — isn't that the sign of organic communication with nature?

foliage ...

The small leaves of a "Sauvageonne"(1); The
large imposing ones of "Grand Siècle"(2), whose young carmine-red
shoots announce more flowers to come; Rosa rugosa and its
crimped foliage (3); almost bluish for "Souvenir d'Amour Violet"(4);
young yellow shoots of "Souvenir de Marcel Proust"(5); Simplicity for "Centenary
of Lourdes" (6); "Tobago"(7), the most original: spear-shaped, serrated, half-
closed leaves assuming all the shades of red and green ...
What variety ... and what concern for harmony !

How often the sensiti-
vity acquired in the
woods has helped
me in my everyday
life and in my
relations with others!
And as for you roses, Monet,
Gauguin, Cézanne, haven't
I been able to recognize you among
a crowd of other roses? Even when you were only a
baby flower, the size of a cornflower, and other
people remained indifferent to your distinction.

WHAT A SCHOOL NATURE IS! WHAT AN EDUCATION!
But to absorb it all you have to educate your senses. We all possess them by nature...
but is there an educational system for developing them? Wasn't that the aim of those
old schoolmasters who regularly took their students for walks in the school of nature?...
    Unfortunately, that's out of fashion now.
However, flowers and plants are mediators in the "return to nature" as I conceive
of it. Their shapes, colours and scents appeal to all the senses.
    This is an EDUCATION OF SENSIBILITY.

The fantastic story of plants and flowers enables us to understand
the evolution of life on earth. It is a LESSON OF NATURE, which offers us lessons
in wisdom. The author Jean-Marie Pelt speaks of "the fabulous history of the
ascent of life, of the rise of sap in one of the main branches of the genealogical
tree of the living world, the Kingdom of plants. A history which reveals
the genius of the organization of living things, the logic of their
structures, their hierarchies, their chronologies, their mechanisms
and their laws".

This opens up a great debate. We are aware now of the necessary
interaction between the two hemispheres of the brain:
— right : sensibility, vision, intuition.
    (Our educators shun these major powers.)
— left : language, abstraction, deduction.
    (Our educators put the emphasis on these powers
    of thought.)
One could say that our brains function at only half of
their capacity. What we need is to mobilize the means
to restore the brain to its
original function.

SENSIBILITY EDUCATION

This means the re-education of
the right hemisphere of the brain.
But sensibility requires a realm
in which to manifest itself.
And this is provided by flowers
and plants, nature in its
broadest sense, which helps us
to open up the paths that lead
to a sensuous understanding
of the phenomenon of life.

It is the history of plants and
flowers that clarifies not only
the origins of this phenomenon
but also the evolution of the
human species.

Here is a paradox.
We cannot educate the sensibility unless we have access
to the living domain of nature.
And we cannot receive the
TEACHINGS OF NATURE if our
sensibility is not open to it.

Sauzet Woods,
21 July 94

43

"Centenary of Lourdes"
pink
The rose-garden at Malicorne.
22 July, 9·30 p.m.
When I sit at the foot of one
of these weeping rose-bushes,
I feel as if I am at the
entrance to the nave of a
cathedral. Their foliage shuts
out the sky to form a pink and
blue vault. There is a feeling
of humility, of peace,
a need for silence.

The sun sinks and the shadows of
these pillars become gigantic.
If you should pass near the Malicorne
rose-gardens one day in July, perhaps
you will come in and share
these emotions with me?

bergamot
jasmine
scent

44

"Centenary of Lourdes"
red

"Centenary of Lourdes" needs
no introduction.

It is a grand classic, which
has now been joined by one of its brothers, whose
petals are a luminous, vibrant red, softened at
just the right places by a few narrow strokes of white.
They are both irresistible.

45

Lake of Joneras, behind the fields
of rootstocks for grafting roses.
23 July 94

46

Propagating

What about total potentiality?
Here is the basic distinction between the vegetable and animal kingdoms.
Put simply, it is the theoretical capacity of any vegetable cell to change as it multiplies
and thereby reconstruct a whole plant, whereas, as we know, animal cells — except
for those of the embryo — can reproduce only themselves as they multiply.

As gardeners, we use this facility to propagate the varieties of roses which we have selected. This is called grafting and takes place in July.

From a branch of the variety we wish to propagate, we cut out a bud in the shape of a shield and insert it under the bark of a wild rose's collar. Grown from seed, this rootstock is chosen for its rooting and vegetation qualities.

In February the wild rose is pruned back to just above the grafted "shield"; which will soon develop in order to turn itself in due course into a rose-bush, whose aboveground growth will be identical to the mother plant.

Creating, selecting and propagating : this is a long task that takes patience, expertise and imagination.
But this is the way gardeners, artisans of nature, supply a soul to the roses they create.

47

" Madame Georges Delbard "

This rose was meant for you, Mother.
 Like you, it has those virtues of the past
that have almost vanished. It may not
 be especially fragrant, but it has a
 certain discreet distinction, an
 irreproachable colour, and it is so
 long-lasting in a vase !
 But seriously, it represents the struggles
 of a lifetime, your husband's intimately
 linked with your own, and now
 shared by your sons.

For before you became the most widely propagated rose for cutting, it took many long years to learn, first of all, how to make you grow "in vitro", since you seemed to be completely intractable to grafting. But then, after a great deal of time and effort, horticulturists were persuaded that, although you might produce few roses per square meter, they made up in quality what they lacked in quantity.

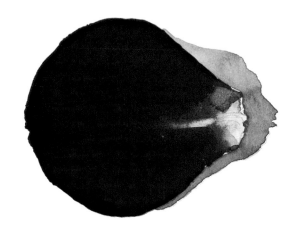

It was comforting to receive great help from the customers who were quick to make the distinction. But life is not all sweetness and light. This rose had barely reached the heights when its success invited fraudulent propagation in South America! The time has come to find that other Madame Delbard who, fortified by experience, will be able to correct her minor defects! A little more scent, perhaps?

49

"Empress Farah"

This is a fairy-tale which began when a rose called "Vivre" won a prize at the Douai-la-Fontaine competition; the royalties on its sales were to be turned over to a foundation for problem children, whose president was Empress Farah of Iran.

Then there was a meeting at the Trianon Palace in Versailles between my father and Her Imperial Majesty in June 1974, the establishment of an orchard of 6,000 hectares in northern Iran and, in spite of the terrible political events, the beginning of a close friendship. Because of its beauty and distinction, our whole family wished to dedicate this rose to the Empress.

The exceptional elegance of the rose is due to its perfect shape, but even more it is the position and importance of the white which ennobles the carmine red that edges its petals.

"Château de Versailles" achieves the same elegance through the slightly silvery white that appears on the reverse side of its petals. The combined effect of these two colours - white and blood red - gives it a more masculine look.

When planted in wide borders, the flowers of "Château de Versailles" sparkle like those aliminum bands that are used to scare off birds.

It makes a grand spectacle.

"Château de Versailles"

rose
pear
scent of "Empress Farah"

Ancinet, 23 July 94, evening

"Mamy Blue"

Is there a more beautiful combination of colours than that of sea, sun and sky?
Azure sea, stormy sea, blazing sun, reddening sun, pure sky, stormy sky...
And always the sun illuminating the depths as the yellow illuminates the blue.
But just as the sky and sea give depth to the sun's rays, the blue expands
the visual boundaries.

"Mamy Blue"

citronella
geranium, ylang ylang
violet, hay
heliotrope

"Dioressence"

"Ô Sole Mio"

"Mamy Blue" the sea,
"Dioressence" the sky, or maybe the reverse — it doesn't really matter. "Ô Sole Mio" always lights up the one or the other with its warm tones and diffuses a light aroma of rose and fruit in the wake of geranium and the likes of ylang ylang.

"Ô Sole Mio"
grapefruit
rose
pineapple, pear
ginger, cinnamon
lichen

"Dioressence"
bergamot
geranium
moss, wood

53

Rose gardens
Gardens of fragrances, colours
                and textures.

"La Faille", Malicorne, 24 July 1994.
Borders of "Perle Noire" roses set off the
wide rows of "Grand Nord"

Arnaud Maurières and Eric Ossart designed for me a garden organized around the scents of roses. Its aim is multicultural in shape, gardens, odours and ingredients.

Many perfumes are built around floral notes, and that of the roses in particular. The square, that resolutely modern shape, makes it possible to work in modules, and to give rhythm to scents and colours

— Floral harmony for the heart of the garden. Floral-scented roses: "Grand Siècle"; "Centenary of Lourdes"; "Lavender Dream". A palette of white, pink and green, with a wisp of blue. Gardens of the West with paths of damp grass.

— Spicy harmony. "Paul Gauguin", "Paul Cézanne", "Ô Sole Mio". Summer colours: yellow, orange, red. Scents of heathland: pelargonium, sage, lupine, catmint, lantana.
Andalusian gardens: herring-bone brick paths, earthenware pots.

— Oriental harmony. Aromatic, balsamic, woody notes: "Dioressence", "Manny Blue". A wealth of mauves, violets, purples and crimsons: heliotropes, stocks, lupines, peonies. Gravel paths.
A Hesperidean harmony would have done just as well: tonic, refreshing, white, yellow, acid. "Souvenir de Marcel Proust", "Ô Sole Mio"; thyme, lavender, orange-trees in tubs.

54

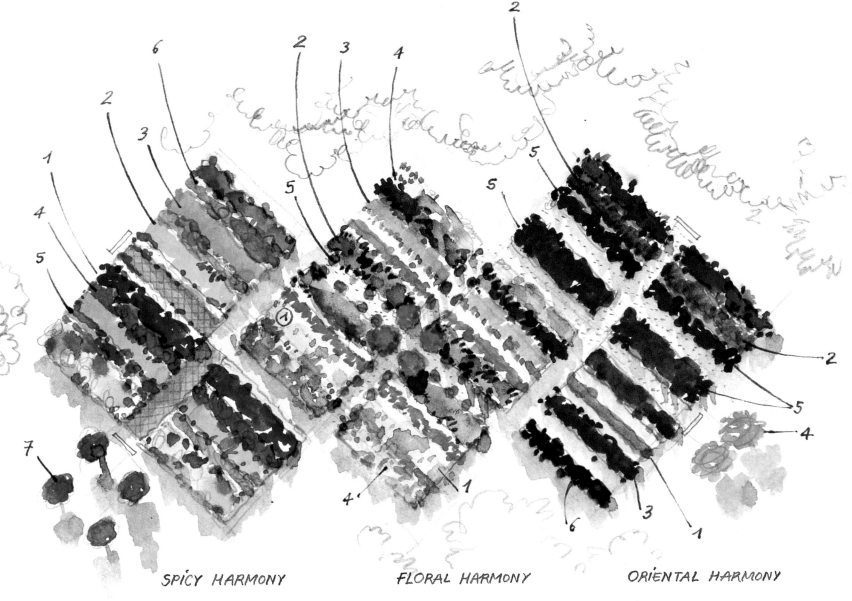

SPICY HARMONY

1 : "Paul Gauguin"
2 : "Paul Cézanne"
3 : "Ô Sole Mio"
4 : Catmint
5 : Sage
6 : Lantana
7 : Cypresses

FLORAL HARMONY

1 : "Grand Siècle"
2 : "Centenary of Lourdes"
3 : "Lavender Dream"
4 : Lilac
5 : Violets

ORIENTAL HARMONY

1 : "Mamy Blue"
2 : "Dioressence"
3 : Peruvian heliotrope
4 : Daturas in pots
5 : Red and purple lupine
6 : Peonies

55

A beneficial, beautiful, benevolent garden

Since the Middle Ages, fruit trees have been the soul of the French garden.
Cultivated first for food, then for decoration, their branches, blossoms and fruit
mark the seasons and the layout of the garden.
  In response to a command of Louis XIV, who wanted his fruit trees to be as
beautiful in winter as in summer, Monsieur de la Quintinie, the inventor of
several devices used in arboriculture, raised them to the level of vegetal sculpture.
For me they are both the emblem and the culmination of the genius of
                    French gardening.

56

When planted around fruit trees,
rose-bushes add softness and colour to
their architectural shapes.

Speak of fruit and you speak of taste. But to taste properly you need to
understand the seasons and the regions and how to search out the native
products of the soil.
Think of the harmonies between the colours of a landscape and the flavours,
the crispness or the richness of a cooked dish. These are harmonies which define
"the right taste", the taste that delights us.

One quick glance is enough to make you remember the intense but very delicate colour. Close your eyes, bury your nose in the heart of "Graham Thomas", and like a hunting dog sniff out the fragrances hidden behind each petal.

Orange-blossom
Cyclamen

scent

fennel
wood,
lichen,
moss, patchouli,
fern, mushroom...

"Graham Thomas"

You will imagine yourself transported into the midst of a wood, on a day in autumn when, after a rainfall, the warm sun reheats the humus, the moss, the lichen and the mushrooms. This is my woodland rose.

"Fair Bianca"

This one I call my little hussy, because she
seems to me half angel, half demon.
Her virginal colour is as strong as the sensuality
of her perfume. First a few notes of
anise, narcissus and syringa;
then, when your head is
reeling, the more secret,
animal smells of musk and
civet.

"Fair Bianca" is the rosegrower's
aphrodisiac

aniseed, anise, basil
narcissus, syringa
hyacinth, grass
musk, civet, heliotrope

scent

"Abraham Darby"

scent

citronella
rose
new-mown hay
apricot, grapefruit
litchi

Warm colours, soft colours.
The great number of its petals, the
richness and density of its
colouring, its chalice-like shape
all make it clear that this has
to do with an offering. With delight
in his eyes, Bacchus confirms that
this is the case, recognizing
those fruity, floral notes that
characterize his St-Pourçain wine
from the Domaine de la Croix d'Or…
And he passes back and forth from rose
to wine until he's drunk!

Sauzet Woods,
The West corner of my little house:
"Abraham Darby" adorns a vine
of chasselas grapes.

60

This light but structured composition casts shadows on my cellar door.

The scented bouquet I have just "tasted" at sunset is equally well structured.
The rose and citronella notes of "Dune".
Lavender scent; the heavy, heady notes of wisteria.

A little breeze, a rise in humidity — and a new "cocktail" is created in which the expert "noses" will rediscover the rich balance of head, heart and base.

The bright yellow, delicate, slightly cone-shaped flowers of "Dune" provide the perfect transition from the hot summer light into the dark coolness of the cellar.
How happy the wine must be in there!

61

scent ▲ citronella rose

"Dune" climbing rose (yellow)
"Munstead" lavender
chinese wisteria

" Salammbô "

Son of " Climbing Delbard " and " Perle Noire ", the touchy, arrogant " Salammbô "
draws together the ochre-coloured gritstone and the almost coal gray of the old
barn door.

Clematis x jackmanii'

... My little house ...

Another perfect partnership : " Parure d'Or", with its frail yellow petals fringed
with carmine, gives the impression that its only aim is to adorn this doll's house.
The deep bluish violet flowers of the clematis punctuate and enliven the
sweetness of the scene.

And can roses be eaten?

It was thanks to Michel Bras, the great chef of the famous
restaurant of Laguiole, that I experienced my first "tasting"
sensations. Then, following Bras's tips, Michel Rubod, an
innkeeper at Commentry, near Malicorne, became a party to
my theme lunches.

   Here are a few recipes based on roses that he thought up and
enjoyed in my house at Ancinet. And I would add that the
quality and conviviality of those meals were also due to the
          gracefulness and hospitality of my wife Anne.
For a starter, try a small salad of arugula and
yellow cherry tomatoes (lukewarm), dressed with oil and
          "Claude Monet" vinegar.

"Fêtes Galantes" butter

Proust butter

Zucchini flowers, mussel stock with "Marcel Proust"
  and "Fêtes Galantes" butter

Ancinet, 26 July 1994

Stuff flowers with poultry mousse or zucchini purée, then steam.
  Rose-butter: soften butter and mix with chopped rose-petals.
Serve flowers in mussel stock blended with rose-butter and
braced with a dash of white wine.

Salmon meunière with lemon juice in a warm cream sauce,
tarragon and " Cézanne" rose petals

———

Melt butter in pan. Lightly coat salmon in seasoned flour. Fry gently
without browning. Remove salmon and keep warm. Add lemon
juice and a pinch of sugar to pan. Add one tablespoonful of cream,
bring to the boil and stir in the mixture of tarragon and
rose petals previously blended with butter.

"Mitsouko" rose brandy

Steep your "Mitsouko" petals in a neutral, fruit-based brandy for at least three weeks. Use 100 g of sugar for 100 g of rose petals. Pour over your sorbet (lime, strawberry, raspberry) and decorate with a few "Mitsouko" petals before serving.

Sorbet of apples and crushed ice
with white wine and "Mitsouko" petals
The apples are simply put through the food-processor and the sorbet-maker.
The sorbet can also be served surrounded by crystallized "Mitsouko"
petals to accompany a lemon tart or apple fritters.

citronella
rose
grapefruit, apricot,
peach, litchi

scent

"Papi Delbard"

Perhaps the most beautiful, the most fragrant and in any case the most complex of all, the achievement of a lifetime devoted to roses. At long last, at the age of 90, my father, Georges Delbard, has his very own rose. And he chose it himself. Still full of life and enthusiasm, he decided that a climbing rose would suit him best.
So there it is, full of perfume and vigour.
A surprising mixture of

My father's garden

youth, character and qualities that have been a long time in the making. A rose that grows tall and strong, to produce a multitude of blossoms and emanate a powerful, generous fragrance – a real fruit cocktail in complete harmony with the warm colours in which the flowers will deck themselves throughout its existence, year in, year out.

69

70

The lessons of nature, instruction of sensibility : here is a new philosophy which teaches us the wisdom of life. BIOSOPHY : that's what I and my old teacher Henri Charnay decided to call it. This suggests that people may recover the wisdom of life by cultivating our earth as gardeners of five senses. To enjoy fulfilment in the health of nature should not be a luxury restricted to a privileged minority, but a right of the people of the whole world.

The first of the Rights of Man is the RIGHT OF NATURE. Our first duty is to behave as temporary owners of the land, careful to leave a world in which life is worth living to the generations of the third millennium. That's what is meant by respect for Creation : honouring the rights of nature, for that is humanity's only hope.

The rose has been offered to us to open our sensibility, our hearts, our imagination, the rose to which the gardener of five senses has added soul, the rose which is ephemeral, but renewed each year,

the rose, which has become the "place of memory", as Elie Wiesel defines it, and helps us to share in so many emotions !

Weren't you created to teach us the lesson of death through life ?

Henri Delbard's advice for successful rose growing

Roses are simple to grow if you follow my five recommendations:
- Don't think twice about purchasing an ample supply of first-rate topsoil: this is the most effective course of action you can take to ensure vigorous and healthy plant growth.
- If a rosebush is late in showing new growth after planting or winter pruning, cover it with a polyethylene bag (which should be pierced several times). This will act as a mini-greenhouse in stimulating and protecting the plant.
- Remember, to combat disease, preventive treatments are better than cures
- For continuous flowering, there are two essential things to do: remove all wilted flowers and water constantly, without breaks, to avoid stressing the plant.
- Prune rosebushes. This is easy to do, for in most cases all you need to do is to cut them back at the end of the winter, leaving 3 or 4 eyes, and take care to remove all small branches.

Translated from the French by Edward Lucie-Smith, Tony Burstall and Michael England; translation coordinated by Stanley Baron

Library Congress Catalog Card Number: 96 84215

ISBN 0 8109 3786 7

Copyright © 1994 Georges Delbard S.A. Editeur,
16, quai de la Mégisserie
75001 Paris, France

Published in 1996 by Harry N. Abrams, Incorporated, New York

A Times Mirror Company

Published in Great Britain under the title *A Passion for Roses*

Printed and bound in Italy